All-Age
Worship

by
Anne Barton
Parish Deacon, Burley, Hants.

gb GROVE BOOKS LIMITED
Bramcote   Nottingham   NG9 3DS

CONTENTS

Copyright Anne Barton 1993

BV
15
.B36
1993

THE COVER PICTURE

is by Andrew Barton

First Impression October 1993

ISSN 0144-1728
ISBN 1 85174 249 2

INTRODUCTION

All-age worship is becoming an increasingly common feature of the corporate life of the local church. The impetus towards the introduction of all-age worship is widespread, as can be seen from the popularity of workshops and training courses on the subject. Recent publications[1] have developed material suitable for all-age worship. Recognition of the need for such material has resulted in an outline structure for these services being brought to Synod for authorization, which will make 'A Service of the Word'[2] an alternative to Morning and Evening Prayer.

However, the introduction of all-age worship can be fraught with practical difficulties, and may highlight tensions between those with differing concepts of church worship. The initial concern is usually with the provision made for children. Yet all-age worship is far more than just a new name for children's work. It is one outworking of a richer understanding of what it means for a local church to be the body of Christ in a particular place.

For many churches the move towards all-age worship has arisen as a response to the perceived needs of the congregation and the community rather than as a more abstract decision, still less because it is seen to be a fashionable trend. What makes all-age worship worthy of attention is that it has proved to be an important step for churches of different types and in very different situations.

For instance, a thriving suburban church is likely to be attracting a large number of nuclear families, and will have a proportionately large number of young children. It is in this type of church, particularly the evangelical churches, that one type of Family Service has developed. However, in these churches there is often concern about the effect of majoring on Family Services for the nurture of the adult congregation. Such a service may indeed be more intelligible for those new to Christian worship, but seems like 'over-age, over-size Sunday School'[3] to others. The plea is therefore for a form of worship that includes the adults as well as the children, so that those of all ages are enabled to worship.

Other churches, especially those in rural areas, may find that the small number of children present means that children of differing ages are grouped together. This can lead the church to examine the ways in which those whose faith is at different stages learn from one another and worship together. If this results in an extension of that principle to include the adult congregation, then the church is moving towards all-age worship.

The widespread acceptance of the Parish Communion across the spectrum of the Church of England has done much to break down the barriers of suspicion caused by differing practice. It has also meant that the

[1] *Patterns for Worship* (GS 898, CHP, 1989; revised edition 1994). *The Promise of His Glory* (CHP, 1990, 1991). Michael Perham, *Enriching the Christian Year* (SPCK, 1993).
[2] *A Service of the Word* (GS 1037A, CHP, 1993).
[3] Myrtle Langley, *Equal Woman* (Marshalls, 1983), p.169, quoted by Francis Bridger, *Children Finding Faith* (SU, 1988), p.145.

likelihood of children being present at communion services has increased. In such a situation a church is forced to examine questions about the status of children within the body of Christ, and to consider how those of all ages can worship together.

There has been a trend towards condensing Sunday worship into the morning, leaving the afternoon free. As a result a church can find itself facing a dearth of adults willing to lead groups for children, when that means they themselves miss the teaching and worship of the adult church. Similarly, leaders may be aware that children are not experiencing the Christian community at worship because their teaching groups happen at the same time as the morning service. Frequently churches have then developed patterns whereby children join the adults for part of the service, or for the whole service on some Sundays. This raises questions about the nature of appropriate worship and teaching, for adults and for children.

It may seem that all-age worship is being presented as a panacea for all the problems facing each and every church! While this is not the case, it is being argued that the fundamental principles underlying all the situations sketched above are basically the same. All are concerned with the composition of the Christian community, including both *adults* and *children*. All are concerned with the development of the members of that community through *teaching*. All are concerned with *worship*, the primary activity of all Christians.

The following three chapters, which form the first part of the booklet, explore the combinations of these four elements of the local church (adults, children, teaching and worship), and how the emphasis varies depending on how the church is structured. To a certain extent, these chapters all cover similar ground but from different starting points. The relevance of each chapter to a particular situation depends how the priorities are perceived. It is likely that one of the three will seem more applicable then the other two, and would seem the most relevant starting point. The other chapters may then add further perspectives. These three chapters are then best viewed as complementary to one another, rather than as a logical sequence of development. Each of these chapters ends with suggestions for initiating discussion about the principles of all-age worship.

Those seeking to introduce all-age worship find that there are considerable obstacles along the way, largely the result of the pre-conceived ideas and assumptions all Christians have about church worship from their own background and experience. It is necessary to allow these to be brought into the open, even though the process may be painful and confusing at times. But it is as hearts and minds are opened to the developing relationship between God and his people, that the vision is caught of what it means to be the community of faith. 'Being a Christian' becomes an adventurous journey, rather than a static state:'Here we have no lasting city, but we seek the city which is to come. Through him then let us continually offer up to God a sacrifice of praise to God, that is, the fruit of lips that acknowledge his name.' (Hebrews 13. 15-16)

PART A: MODELS AND TENSIONS

1. SCHOOL, FAMILY OR PILGRIM CHURCH?

As a church explores possible ways of developing its life and ministry, particularly in regard to the place of all-age worship, it is helpful to have some way of analyzing its present position. The 1988 Report *Children in the Way*[1] makes a useful starting point for such a discussion. The Report describes the structure of churches in terms of three models which have been predominant in the last century, and therefore within the lifetime of existing churchgoers. An objective examination of the functioning of these models can bring to light the assumptions upon which present patterns of church life and worship are based.

Within any congregation there will be those whose experience is of one or more of the different models in operation. Not only does the model vary from place to place and church to church, but also from time to time. This means that the person brought up in St Agatha's in the 1960s is likely to have experienced a different model from that known to the person brought up there in the 1930s, and neither may recognize the model in operation in the 1990s. All bring different basic assumptions to the consideration of all-age worship.

The School model
Historically, the first of the three models was the 'School'. It is this that has been responsible for the widely held view that adults and children are to be treated differently and separately within the church.

The School model of nurture has its roots in the Sunday School movement. This began over 100 years ago with the thoroughly laudable intention of providing basic education for children who would not otherwise have received it. At the same time, they received a thorough grounding in the Scriptures. It was widely successful, so much so that the name 'Sunday School' is still a generic term that covers children's activities within the church. The 1991 Report *All God's Children?*[2] estimates that over two thirds of the nation's children were in the Sunday Schools of the 1930s and 1940s, and that even in the mid-1950s the figure was still about half.

Given such widespread influence, it is not surprising that many adult members of congregations in the 1990s have the School model of nurture as their own working model for the nurture of children within the church. Particularly among those over 40, there will be a substantial majority who experienced Sunday School as children. This is likely to be higher than the proportions given above as a survey[3] indicated.

The implications of a School model of nurture have a profound effect on the understanding and expectation of Christian learning. It is immediately apparent that the School model is an educational one. Such were its origins, and its prime intentions. The terminology of the Sunday School

[1] *Children in the Way* (CHP, 1988).
[2] *All God's Children?* (CHP, 1991), p.4.
[3] *All God's Children?*, p.12.

has always reflected its educational goals. There are 'teachers' and 'classes'. The persistence of such titles shows how deep the acceptance of this particular model is.

In a church operating on a School model of nurture, the child progresses through a series of classes, which are defined by chronological age, emerging at the end of the process to join the adult community. If the task of the adult community is perceived to be worship, then the model has implanted the idea that children are taught and adults worship.

A serious consequence of the School model is that school is something to be abandoned on becoming an adult. The drift away from Sunday School as children grow older may well have more to do with this perception than with a conscious rejection of Christianity. In this case the child learner does not become an adult worshipper.

The formality of the School model may seem to bear too little resemblance to modern educational methods to be applicable. It is however the model that is alive in the memories of adults remembering how they were taught in their childhood when such formal approaches to education were more common, in both school and Sunday School. Because being a leader of children's work in churches is a voluntary activity and training is limited, leaders are more dependent on the memories of their own experience than schoolteachers are. This builds in a conservative approach where earlier methods persist longer than might be expected.

The consequences of a School model for the Christian community as a whole can impose severe limitations. It limits the expectation that children will worship, because it is assumed that their primary task is to learn. It takes for granted that children learn from adults and does not include the expectation of mutual learning. It discourages adults from learning because that is seen to be an appropriate activity for children, not adults.[1]

The impact of the School model on the adults in the community can be profound. Perhaps most seriously it fosters the notion that religion is something one grows out of on reaching maturity, so that many adults dismiss the claims of Christianity without serious consideration. For those who remain, there is a tendency to adopt the attitude of pupils within the School model, replacing the teacher/pupil distinction by an ordained/lay one.

The School model exercises considerable influence on the behaviour patterns expected of children by many church members. This may well reflect their experience as children rather than the present situation. It was common practice for the Sunday School to meet in a different place and at a different time from the normal worship of the congregation. One good reason for the different timing was so that Sunday School teachers were not excluded from worship because of their teaching role. It would be quite possible for adult worshippers and children attending Sunday School to be unaware of the other's existence, let alone making any connection between the two. Church worship would be an adult affair; few

[1] For further reading, see J. M. Hull, *What prevents Christian adults from learning?*, (Trinity Press International, 1991).

children would be present and those that were would be expected to be utterly unobtrusive. Such memories will often lie behind the attitude that children are a distraction in church and therefore not welcome.

The use of a model that is primarily didactic has built into it an assumption of a Christian culture, in which children are taught the faith in childhood and graduate to the worshipping life of the adult community. This means that churches working on such a model tend to separate adults and children, and treat them differently. The expectation is that children learn, whereas adults worship. If this distinction is recognized to be inappropriate, too rigid an adherence to the School model may determine the ways in which development is possible. The children's' programme is widened to include some worship; the adult members of the church are encouraged to participate in study groups, and preaching is equated with teaching. However, the reluctance to have adults and children engaged in worship together will persist, and there is little recognition of a mutual learning process.

The Family model

The 1950s and 1960s saw a marked decline in Sunday School attendance, which forced the churches to look critically at the way in which children were treated. As the weaknesses became apparent, churches began to adapt their priorities to meet the changed social climate in which they were living. Out of this was derived the Family model. In many churches there is, at least once a month, a service that declares itself in some way to be 'Family'. A number of factors contributed to this change in emphasis. Many of these were sociological and pragmatic rather than explicitly theological.

The late 1950s and 1960s saw an increase in material affluence after the austerity of the previous decades. Ownership of cars and televisions became commonplace. With such trends went an increased privatisation of social life. Attendance at football matches declined; cinemas closed; social mobility increased, particularly among the middle classes where the church tended to make more impact than among the working class. The significance of the extended family and the community diminished, to be replaced by the nuclear family.

The attitude to Sunday as a day to be kept holy has changed. It has come to be regarded as a day of recreation, for pursuing leisure interests, rather than a day of rest on sabbatarian principles. This change is reflected in the way that for many Christians church activities are confined to Sunday morning, or morning and evening, whereas Sunday Schools traditionally met in the afternoon.

The perception of Sunday as a day for leisure pursuits affected attitudes to Sunday School. The situation is radically different from the early days of the Sunday School Movement. Then children who worked were able to come to Sunday School for education. In a society where compulsory education is taken for granted, that need no longer exists. As a result, the way in which education is categorized has changed. For children, school is their work, as opposed to something to be done in leisure time. If their participation in the life of the church is portrayed as 'Sunday School' then there will be resistance to that encroaching upon a day for leisure. This is particularly pronounced for children whose parents and peer group have no Christian commitment.

As a response to the very different environment in which the church now found itself, the Family model began to emerge to replace the School model. Because the various Sunday church activities were condensed into the morning, leaving the rest of the day free for other pursuits, adults and children came to church at the same time. The awareness of the church as a Christian community comprising both adults and children grew. At the same time, increased social mobility meant that relatives might be widely scattered. The nuclear family of 'Mum, Dad and the kids' was seen as the norm, so much so that became the generally understood definition of 'family'. (A Family ticket usually means two adults and two children.) A local church would find that a substantial part of its membership consisted of a number of nuclear family units, living in the same locality as other nuclear families with whom the church had little contact. In such circumstances, the Family model for the church would be likely to predominate.

One strength of the Family model is that such a church recognises that it has within it both adults and children, even though it is likely to assume the Western nuclear family as an ideal, to the exclusion of others. The development of the corporate life of that community, particularly when it meets together on a Sunday, will follow one of two strands depending on whether it gives priority to worship or to teaching. This is examined in the following chapter.

The Pilgrim Church model

The School and Family models have within them inadequacies (as indeed will any model). These centre around two issues. One is whether adults and children are all recognized as part of the one Christian community. The other is whether worship is emphasized at the expense of teaching, or *vice versa*, and the related issue of whether opportunities for both worship and teaching are provided for both adults and children.

If there is a model that encourages the development of both adults and children through worship and through teaching, then such a model deserves attention. This is what the Report *Children in the Way*[1] chose to describe as the 'Pilgrim Church', and it is this model that is generally described as all-age worship.

'Imagine a group of people of all ages going for a long walk together. At times the children and adults will walk along together, talking as they go, sharing stories with first one person and then another, each observing different things and sharing their discoveries. At times the children will lag behind and some of the adults will have to wait for them or urge them on. Sometimes the smallest children may ask to be

[1] *Children in the Way*, CHP, (1988), p.33.

8

carried. At other times, though, the children will dash ahead making new discoveries, and may, perhaps, pull the adults along to see what they have found. Some adults may well behave like these children, of course. For all there will be times of progress and times of rest and refreshment, time to admire the view, and times of plodding on, and the eventual satisfaction of arrival at their destination.

'Of course, a pilgrimage is something more than a hike. Traditionally it is a group of people of all kinds and all ages united in reaching a common goal.'[1]

The vision of the 'Pilgrim Church' is captured by this illustration. It caters for worship and teaching for both adults and children, allowing each to take priority as necessary without building a model in which the priorities are set. Children and adults are both present, together or separate as need demands. There is learning, both for children and adults, without the assumption that the children will be always be the learners and the adults the teachers. There is worship for both adults and children, by virtue of being on a shared journey to a common goal, without expecting that the adults will always be ahead of the children.

The use of the Pilgrim church model requires a considerable change in the way members of a congregation approach their life together. It is a comparatively recent development, which means that those involved in its implementation will be helped by being able to re-examine and to be aware of the alternative models that they have previously used.

Suggestions for groups
It is not easy for any individual Christian to examine the pre-suppositions on which their expectations of church life are based, still less to articulate them. Nevertheless, such expectations will affect their understanding of the place of all-age worship.

The members of the group can be encouraged to reminisce about their own experience, particularly as children. This may reflect different cultures, different classes and different denominations, as well as the three models outlined above.

Pictures can be drawn to illustrate the different models of church. This has the advantage of involving those less willing to talk in a group, and can be very revealing. It is also possible to link this to drawing the way in which a local church is seen to be working. This can be a way of discovering together how a church is perceived.

An examination of the names used for services and for children's activities can be enlightening. This should include both official names and popular usage. For example, the name 'Sunday School' may persist long after the group has been called something else. 'Family Service' may be spoken of as 'The children's service'. Locally devised names may convey nothing to those who are not regular worshippers at that church, and result in the persistence of names previously used.

[1] *Children in the Way*, CHP, (1988), *op. cit.*

9

Church architecture is closely linked to the assumptions of a particular model for the life of a Christian community. A traditional church building encourages the passivity of the congregation. A traditionally built non-conformist chapel gives pride of place to the ministry of the word. A church built in the round, such as the Roman Catholic Cathedral in Liverpool, owes much to the Family model. As influences on architecture take some time to become apparent, there are as yet few buildings that reflect the Pilgrim Church; the adventurous Portsmouth Cathedral is one. A discussion of the effect of various church buildings on the self-image of the Christian community can be a profitable starting point.

2. WORSHIP AND TEACHING

Both worship and teaching form part of the agenda for the corporate life of the Christian community so that it would be difficult to imagine a church in which either of these was completely excluded. Nonetheless, one may be emphasized at the expense of the other, so that this becomes an overriding factor in determining the priorities in the church's corporate activity.

Worship
Worship has to be at the heart of the life of every individual Christian and at the heart of the life of the Christian community gathered together. It is the appropriate expression of the relationship into which they have entered as children of our heavenly Father. If worship is not the central, abiding passion of Christians, then they are in danger of dethroning God from his rightful place, and putting something else there instead. It may be something that deserves considerable attention—for example, a concern for social action or for evangelism—but even these should derive from a relationship with God rather than be a substitute for it.

Worship is the activity of heaven. It will persist even in eternity,[1] where it will be the expression of a love that never ends. Our worship now is at best a foretaste to what is to come. It should be 'a door standing open in heaven'.[2] If Christians are satisfied now with worship that does not engage their hearts and minds and lift them heavenward, it makes it harder to believe that they look forward to the prospect of eternal life with much enthusiasm.

As children grow, their parents and other adults concerned with their nurture seek to introduce them to the world around then in all its dimensions. Their physical, mental and emotional development is a source of much parental pride. Correspondingly, the spiritual development of children is to be nurtured and encouraged. To attempt this without giving children space to respond to God in worship is to place unnecessary and unhelpful limitations upon them.

If children are not given the opportunity to be part of the worshipping community, it is not only they who suffer. The adults miss out too. Children know that they are naughty, make mistakes, need to be picked up and set back on their feet. Adults find that difficult to accept in themselves. Children are capable of exuberant, spontaneous outbursts of love, praise and thanksgiving, where adults are often too restrained. Children know that they are frail and dependent. Adults too often pretend that they are not. But 'unless you turn and become like children, you will never enter the kingdom of heaven.'[3] The whole Christian community benefits from acknowledging children as part of that community.

[1] 1 Corinthians 13.8.
[2] Revelation 4.1.
[3] Luke 18.3

Teaching

Teaching has long been viewed as an essential part of the Christian community's life. It is the means by which the story of the incarnate God, of his involvement with his world, is passed from person to person and from generation to generation. Without teachers in the Christian community there would not be the means for the community to work out the implications of that story for their own lives. The Christian community needs God's gift of teachers just as it needs evangelists and prophets, for the building up of the body of Christ.[1]

Churches have needed to address the question of who should be taught. In the wake of the Sunday School Movement there was a tendency to think that teaching was to be equated with instruction and was appropriate for children rather than for adults. This fitted well within a Church of England that still looked back to the era of Christendom in its liturgy. Cranmer had no need of a service for adult baptism, but assumed that all children were baptized in infancy. His vision was that all children would then be instructed in the faith as they grew. At the same time, he had an intellectual's expectation of self-motivated adult learning. Adults would 'read, mark, learn and inwardly digest'; the role of the preacher was to expound scripture and so enable this process. In this way, for the adults, preaching and teaching are identified. The effect of this can be to limit both the scope of preaching and that of teaching.

The changed social climate has meant a different attitude to adult learning in the church. There are now many adults whose childhood experience of the Christian church is either very limited or non-existent. Younger adults may not even have received much through school assemblies and religious education. As such people are drawn towards Christian commitment, there is a need for basic instruction to be available to adults.

There is an accurate perception that children in the church community still need to learn the basics of the faith in which it is hoped they will live and grow. A place undoubtedly exists for handing on to them the story of salvation history. The names, places and events need to become familiar. There is a place for teaching practical skills; for instance, children will be helped by learning the skills of finding their way around the Bible. But the tendency to limit educational horizons to the acquisition of information has been questioned. Such methods make little connection with other aspects of a child's life. The result may all too often be a child who *knows about Jesus* in an academic sense in the context of education, but who does not *know Jesus* in the context of the believing community.

As educational methods have changed and developed, the validity of different methods of teaching has come under scrutiny. In schools 'chalk and talk' is supplemented, if not supplanted, by work which requires more active participation, often by working in groups. Churches need to look critically at the educational techniques they are using and be prepared to adapt them if necessary. A traditional sermon is after all just 'talk' without even the 'chalk'. In the context of all-age worship, other approaches can be equally profitable. The question that needs to be asked is whether people

[1] Ephesians 4.11.

are learning, rather than whether they are being taught. If the teaching methods used are not interactive, and if there is no opportunity for feedback then teachers have little idea of the effect of their teaching.

The style of Family services that has been introduced indicates whether a church puts worship or teaching as the higher priority. Such services have developed along two different lines, depending largely on the traditions of a particular church. One line tends to a non-eucharistic Family service where teaching and children are paramount; the other tends to a Family communion more concerned with adults and worship.

Priority given to teaching
In churches of an evangelical tradition, teaching would be given a high priority. The Word would predominate, rather than the Sacraments. The sermon would be the focal point of the services; it is not unusual even now for such churches to advertise their services by giving the name of the preacher and the subject of the sermon. The impossibility of a short Family Service containing a lengthy expository sermon would be advanced as an argument against a regular pattern of Family Services. Such a church would be more inclined to have children present at the beginning of the service rather than 'coming in for a blessing' at the eucharist.

It was however in churches that have a concern for evangelism that the non-eucharistic Family Service developed. This was from a determination to have something aimed at attracting those on the fringes of the church which was intelligible to them, yet made a clear presentation of the claims of Christ. The CPAS book *Family Worship* (1971) is an example of the type of service that became popular. The increasing demand for material of this ethos is shown by the expansion of this book into *Church Family Worship* (Hodder and Stoughton, 1988), and was one of the reasons behind *Patterns for Worship* (CUP, 1989). There had been earlier recognition of this need.[1] Yet despite repeated appeals, it is only in 1993 that proposals for an authorized format for such a service have been brought before Synod.[2] The format of Family Services has in the meantime developed independently. The centrepiece of a Family Service is generally a short, didactic 'talk', apparently aimed at 7-10 year olds and amply illustrated with visual aids. The liturgy would be simplified, the children involved in various ways, and the entire proceedings complete within 40-50 minutes.

This type of Family service has been very well received by those who fit the nuclear family model of parents with young children. By seeking to attract young families, the church is fulfilling a need for support felt by adults who find themselves as the parents in a nuclear family deprived by social mobility of the support traditionally given by the extended family and community. It is no coincidence that this type of Family Service has flourished in the new estates of suburbia where such nuclear families predominate. It has been less successful when imposed on communities where the traditional network of support still operates, and in those where even the nuclear family is no longer the norm.

[1] Bryan Spinks, in *The Renewal of Common Prayer*, (CHP, 1993), chapter 7.
[2] *A Service of the Word*, GS 1037A, (CHP, 1993).

The weaknesses that can be apparent in such Family Services are summarized in the Introduction to *Patterns for Worship.*[1] Among these are listed comments that such worship can be 'childish', 'banal', 'superficial', 'dominated by a strong teaching aim'. When Family Services fall into this pattern, the points of reference are likely to be children and teaching, rather than adults and worship. Adults can be cast into the role of passive spectators, rather like parents at a school concert. The effect is to give too high a place to the nuclear family, at the expense of the awareness of the church as a family. This can make those who are for instance single, bereaved, elderly, divorced, or childless feel less accepted as part of the church family.

Overall, this pattern of the Family Service has become established in churches that give priority to teaching, while keeping some balance between teaching and worship. There are churches where the emphasis is very heavily weighted towards teaching. In such churches, if the sermon is seen to be the focal point of the service and the main purpose of the service to be an opportunity for teaching, there will be reluctance to see it changed. In such circumstances the Family Service is unlikely to be more than a once-a-month occasion, at most. The priorities of the church will be apparent in what happens the other weeks. Here the church may well revert to the School model, with children and adults engaged in separate activities.

Priority given to worship

As well as the development of the non-eucharistic Family Service, there has been a parallel change which has brought churches to a similar model from a very different starting point and with different priorities. Here the priorities are seen to be adults and worship, rather than children and teaching. These are churches influenced by the Parish Communion Movement, originally a Catholic Movement within the Church of England. It was this movement that restored the Eucharist to a central place in the worship of the Church, replacing the dual pattern of early communion and a mid-morning sung Eucharist common from the Oxford Movement with the mid-morning Parish Communion.

Since the priority in such a church would be worship rather than teaching, the emphasis is on the Sacraments rather than on the Word. The division between adults and children becomes synonymous with the division between communicant and non-communicant; graduation to adult status comes at confirmation. The Family model for such a church looks to the participation of both adults and children in the Parish Communion service. For the children this would mean encouragement to participate in the liturgy, perhaps by being in the choir or by being servers. There may also be pressure for earlier confirmation.

The sociological changes that favoured the transition to once-a-Sunday attendance in the morning fitted well with the Parish Communion pattern. The trend towards short sermons that is a characteristic of the non-eucharistic Family Service is also found in the Parish Communion, where restricting the length of the sermon is frequently the favoured means of

[1] *Patterns for Worship,* (CHP, 1989), p.2.

keeping a lengthy liturgy within the constraints of limited time. Such constraints become more apparent when the Family model is incorporated into the Parish Communion structure, so that the limited attention span of children is a consideration.

The weakness of the non-eucharistic Family Service was seen to be the high priority given to children and teaching, so that the service has the feel of Sunday school about it. The reverse is the case in the Family Communion. Here the presence of children is accepted though the style of the service makes little concession to them. The concerns are primarily the adults and worship. If the other type of Family Service is at worst Sunday School with adults present, then the Family Communion runs the risk of being simply an adult service with children present.

Suggestions for groups
A group can be encouraged to discuss how they see their church's priorities, with regard to teaching and worship. If there is a Family Service or a Family Communion, discuss where it falls into one of the two patterns described above.

The areas of discontent about family worship will indicate which sections of the church family are being excluded by the pattern of worship. A church will need to consider whether the image it presents of family life is true to scripture, and how that image relates to the community in which the church is placed.

If children come in for only part of the service, consider whether it is at the beginning or the end of the service, and whichever is the pattern, what were the reasons for its adoption. In the light of this, it is possible to initiate discussion about the relative importance of worship and teaching for that church. The experience of those who have seen alternative patterns can work can be valuable.

3. ADULTS and CHILDREN

The principle of all-age worship runs counter to a division of the church into adults and children. In practice, such a sharp division is difficult to make. Are the children those who leave for their own activities partway through the service? Are the teenagers regarded as children or adults? What marks the transition from child to adult? School leaving age? Communicant status? It will be found that the assumptions being made will reflect the models of the church in operation.

Where a church is functioning by modelling itself as a school, the division between adults and children can easily be taken for granted. Those who are at school are seen in one category, those who have left in another. Chronological age becomes the predominant factor in subdividing either adults or children. As at school, children are grouped in classes according to age. Weekday activities for adults can also be categorised by age, so that one group caters for 16-19 year olds, another for those in their 20s, another for the over 70s. Such categorization is frequently successful in bringing together those with similar concerns. However, the married couple in their mid 20s may feel ill at ease in a group that is predominantly singles and seems to them like the youth club they belonged to in their teens. Not every 70 year old is ready to be labelled geriatric and treated accordingly. The School model can also perpetuate division by gender, in a way that used to be commonplace in education, but which would seem strange in schools in the 1990s.

The Family model for a church can also over-emphasise the distinction between adults and children. This can all too easily be done by those whose intention is to welcome the presence of children, but who effectively treat them as a separate species. This can be because of a prominent model of the family as the nuclear family, which subdivides into parents and children. This can result in a service which is a composite of sections for adults and sections for children. For example, to have parts of the service labelled or announced as 'the children's song', or 'the children's talk' implies to them that they are different, and it implies to the adults that they need not take that bit seriously.

For many, confirmation is still seen as a rite of passage from childhood to adulthood. Confirmation has traditionally taken place in early adolescence and from then on the young person was assumed to be an adult member of the worshipping community. In general, confirmation has been the prerequisite for admission to communion. The separation into communicants and non-communicants is in this way seen as equivalent to the separation of adults from children.

The changing composition of the church has called into question the traditional association of confirmation with a particular age group. Increasingly, candidates for confirmation are adults rather than thirteen year olds. This is because an increasing number of the population reach a later age without hearing the gospel and responding to it. Any church that takes evangelism seriously should be reaching out to such people, and so there will be unconfirmed adults at church services. The unconfirmed can no longer be assumed to be just the children below a certain age.

There is pressure against equating the adult worshippers with the confirmed (and therefore communicant) members of the church. Still greater pressure comes when the status of children as members of the household of faith is considered. The scandal of baptizing children as infants, thereby declaring them to be members of God's family the church, and then denying them communion until they are confirmed is one that becomes increasingly apparent once they are present at communion services.[1]

There are then a number of ways in which a division of the church community into adults and children can arise. The impression that is built up is one whereby adults and worship are placed together, as are children and teaching. Such assumptions have a bad effect on the whole of the Christian community. Worship is deemed to be an adult activity. Children are deemed a distraction and an irrelevance. On the rare occasions when they are included in the worship, their presence is either ignored or it is catered for by a children's' slot of juvenile choruses and a patronizing talk. Equally harmful is the assumption that teaching is only suitable for children, that education is something left behind at the end of schooldays.

An over-rigid separation of adults and children can arise in churches which are firmly committed to a teaching ministry. Here teaching is equated with preaching, and expository sermons of considerable length are an important part of Sunday morning. Such sermons are clearly beyond the attention-span of most children, so it seems reasonable to separate them off for teaching appropriate for their age group. The message given is that children are excluded from what adults see as important.

The insistence on chronological age as a means of division is in itself divisive of the body of Christ. It takes little account of the work on faith development done by Fowler and by Westerhoff. This has been summarized in a supplement to the Report *Children in the Way*.[1] This is work which repays more detailed study. However, they contain illustrations that can help to convey the idea of faith development by stages which continue throughout life. This is particularly helpful in providing an alternative model to those who think of the Christian community in terms of adults and children.

Suggestions for groups
It is instructive to examine the provision for the various age groups within the church. In particular, the group should see whether there are cut-off points determined by chronological age, and discuss the extent to which these are appropriate. The place occupied by teenagers is of particular relevance here.

The group should be encouraged to view the architecture and furnishings of the church through the eyes of a child by getting down to their level (literally!). This can initiate discussion of their perception of the church as a community primarily geared for adults, or for children, or both.

[1] For a fuller discussion of this issue, see Daniel Young, *Welcoming Children to Communion*, (Grove Worship Series No. 85 now out of print), and Colin Buchanan, *Children in Communion* (Grove Worship Series No. 112).
[2] How Faith Grows, (CHP, 1991).

PART B: ALL-AGE WORSHIP
4. MAKING THE TRANSITION

The vision of all-age worship and learning is the vision of the church as a pilgrim people. The whole Christian community, regardless of age, needs to be engaged on a journey of faith, learning and worshipping as they go. Depending on the models that have been operating in a local church, this can mean either minor adjustments in an existing pattern, or it may mean a major transition. Even where the apparent changes are slight, these may be the implementation of a fundamental change in attitude. An all-age strategy is by its very nature something that cannot be imposed upon a congregation, as it requires their active participation. The vision needs to be shared and caught for this to happen.

The introduction of an all-age style of worship involves practical considerations, which need to be thought about before changes are made. There needs to be time for assimilation to a different pattern for Sunday morning. Such changes cannot be made overnight, or implemented for a few weeks and then abandoned in despair for lack of planning.[1] Careful forethought and preparation can mean that the scheme does not founder unnecessarily. The issues involved will be specific to each community and church building, but the points outlined below are among those likely to arise.

Syllabus
It has long been the practice for there to be a separate syllabus for the children of the church. This originates from the days of the Sunday School. It has however been perpetuated and implicitly encouraged by those who are most concerned for the education of children in the church. The age group teaching materials produced by Scripture Union and by CPAS are excellent and widely used. However, they are difficult to correlate either to an official Sunday lectionary or to a locally devised scheme. Occasions such as Harvest can throw the pattern out.

It seems that there is no ideal solution to this problem. Scripture Union have worked hard to correlate their teaching material for different age groups and in producing parallel material for all-age worship. It is possible to gear the teaching of the entire church to such a syllabus. This can mean over-riding the requirements of the lectionary, which in some churches would be unacceptable. Others may be concerned that it limits teaching themes to those within the reach of all, so that a detailed week-by-week exposition of Romans is unlikely.

It is possible to gear the themes of worship and teaching to the lectionary. This is the approach taken in books by Sharon Swain[2] and Susan Sayers.[2] However, this is being promoted just as the limitations of the ASB two-year lectionary are being recognized, as is the over-use of the suggested Sunday themes. Future lectionary developments, such as the provision for open and closed seasons of the year, may ease the situation.

[1] For further reading, see Trevor Lloyd in *The Renewal of Common Prayer, op. cit.*, chapter 11.
[2] Sharon Swain, *The Sermon Slot* (SPCK, 1992).
[3] Susan Sayers, *Springboard to Worship*, (Kevin Mayhew, 1989).

Another approach is to abandon the hope of correlation with either lectionary or teaching scheme. This recognizes the reality that an occasional all-age service will attract those on the fringe who are not present on other weeks. Where this is the case, it may be more helpful to view each occasion as a one-off, exploring a basic theme rather than trying to build up a logical sequence. A resource such as Margaret Dean's *Pick and Mix*[1] would be helpful here.

In the light of considering the nature of its programme for teaching and worship, a church will come to conclusions about its vision for the appropriate place for all-age worship in its life. The decision might be to have all the Christian community together on every Sunday. This would probably mean provision for teaching through home groups and age-related midweek activities. It might mean considering a Sunday pattern of teaching groups followed by worship together, as described by Judith Rose.[2] It might mean an all-age service once a month, with other patterns being adopted on other Sundays. To some extent, the decision will reflect the limitations of buildings and leaders. But the decision needs to be made in the light of a desire to be the pilgrim people of God following his leading and trusting in his provision, rather than being weighed down with past assumptions.

It cannot be emphasized too much that, whatever path a church decides to adopt, it needs following through for several months at least. Minor adjustments will need to be made along the way, but the basic pattern needs to be clear and the reasons for its adoption well understood.

Seating
It is worth having a clear idea of how seating will be arranged and used. Here the expectations derived from earlier models may be prominent. Those working to a school-type model may envisage children sitting in classes with their leaders. For such a view it will be argued that this allows small children to be at the front so they can see, while the worship of the adults is less disrupted. It has sometimes been the case that those most in favour of such an arrangement are parents uncertain of their ability to control their children in church. Such parents may need to be enabled to see where their own expectations of their children are unrealistic. In theory such an arrangement caters for children who are sent to church by parents who do not themselves attend. The numbers of such children are far fewer than was once the case, and in practice they are likely to have attached themselves to friends whose parents are present, so that a light, informal sponsoring of such children ensures that they are not overlooked.

The Family model produces different patterns of seating. There will be greater pressure to have seating in the round, or at least a semi-circle, even if the church has not gone through a process of re-ordering. Families will sit as family units, so that there are adults and children scattered throughout the congregation. This is likely to re-enforce the unspoken assumption that the church family is a collection of nuclear families. While this can enhance a warm, informal atmosphere, the effect of alienation on

[1] Margaret Dean, *Pick and Mix*, (NS/CHP, 1992).
[2] Judith Rose, *Sunday Learning for All Ages*, (Grove pastoral Series, No. 11, 1982).

those who do not fit the nuclear family model can be acute. Included in this sense of alienation are teenagers, who do not fit either the role of parent or that of small child. Attempts to include those who do not fit the model can themselves be highly embarrassing and result in a sense of rejection. Part of the preparation for a church that recognizes itself in this description would be for the church to heighten its awareness of the whole church as the family of God, in all the richness of that image.

The all-age pattern of worship would seek to involve the entire congregation in a sense of being the people of God worshipping him together. In such a model, it is not generally helpful to segregate children into a separate area. This produces a sense of isolation from the rest of the community, and deprives children of the help an older member of the community is able to provide. But that older member does not have to be a parent. The church will grow in its awareness of being the people of God together as bonds are built that transcend the nuclear family. This understanding will also alleviate the problem of all-age worship being viewed as 'toddler anarchy'. Of course toddlers who are unaccustomed to worship will find a Sunday morning service strange. Their experience of large buildings and lots of people is very probably of playgroup or a Mums and Toddlers group (which might well happen in the same building as Sunday worship!). Then they are encouraged to run and climb, to jump and shout—so that is what they do. It takes patience and understanding from the Christian community to love and welcome such children, and to bring them and their parents to a sense of God's acceptance of them. At the other end of the scale is the mother whose memories of church worship are of a repressive silence. If she plucks up the courage to bring her baby at all, she will flee in confusion at the first whimper. She too would be helped by a fellow worshipper alongside her, helping to calm both her and the child, communicating to her a sense of their value in the eyes of the Christian community and of God.

Space
A related issue to that of seating is that of space. To assume that the congregation remains in its place is to assume a passive model of worship, as something that is done to those present rather than requiring their active involvement. It is not conducive to corporate worship to cast most of those present into the role of spectator. This can easily be overlooked by those leading worship as their involvement is more active.

This issue is not something new. For many years the principal opportunity for members of a congregation to move about has been when they come forward to receive communion. The active participation involved in 'getting up out of your seat' is itself a positive commitment, as Billy Graham has long realised. In the light of this, it is interesting to consider the effect of receiving communion in one's place. It may then become another aspect of being a passive recipient in worship.

All age worship heightens awareness of the use of space, as it is involves more active participation. Unless it is thought out, more movement can be chaotic. It is, however, an important aspect of worship that requires consideration. There is a great truth in the adage that we remember

10% of what we hear	50% of what we say
30% of what we see	but 90% of what we do.

5. 'A SERVICE OF THE WORD'

Fundamental to the idea of all-age worship is that all those present contribute to the worshipping life of the community. In this way the members of the community build up and encourage one another; the pilgrim people support one another.This can mark a significant change in the way in which corporate worship is perceived by the community. It becomes something in which they are involved, rather than an event at which they are cast in the role of spectators.

This chapter considers ways in which the involvement of the congregation becomes active. Some of this is an extension of practices common in most churches. Even there, the adoption of all-age worship may mean fresh adaptation of existing practice. For others, the changes may seem more radical. Whatever is done, it must arise from the conviction that the church is thereby better enabled to be the people of God offering him their worship and proclaiming Jesus as Lord.

When a community is regularly engaged in a corporate activity, a pattern of behaviour tends to emerge, even if it is never officially recognized. This stability is an important part of corporate worship. The members of the congregation need to be sufficiently at ease to relax and enter wholeheartedly into the worship. This is particularly true of small children who delight in patterns and repetition. There is therefore great value for the spiritual formation of Christian disciples in having a recognizable framework for services.

'A Service of The Word' is the title of the proposals before General Synod in 1993 for authorization as an alternative to Morning or Evening Prayer. It is intended to recognize the type of service that has become a familiar part of the life of many Anglican congregations. In doing so, such services are given an authorized standing. The structure proposed is one designed to retain the flexibility that has characterized such services, while at the same time providing a framework. If widely adopted, it will bring together two strengths of this type of corporate worship. Firstly, it provides scope for the strength of local vitality and enthusiasm. Secondly, it looks beyond the individual congregation to a vision of common prayer; this is significant in providing roots for Christians in a time of mobility.

In order that 'A Service of the Word' can be used as a structure for all-age worship, the principle of active involvement needs to be kept clearly in mind. This will affect all aspects of the worship.

Leadership
All-age worship needs leadership, just as much as any other form of corporate worship. There is a place for a presidential role, whether the worship includes the Eucharist or not. However, solo leadership is unlikely to sit comfortably with all-age worship. It is here that a church will benefit from having a Worship Committee, so that the planning and leadership of worship is shared. The training and expertise of the clergy is needed here, not least because the incumbent of the parish is charged with the responsibility for worship. But the gifts of others are also needed

to put flesh on the skeleton structure of the service; the musicians, the artists, the teachers, the actors, the storytellers. The Worship Committee can be at the hub of planning how such gifts can be used to enable all those present to offer their worship. It is important, particularly in the initial stages, to check continually that the worship really is all ages worshipping; old habits die hard. A planning team is more likely to spot this than leaders working individually. Partly because of the shared nature of such planning, advance preparation becomes necessary. This is something that will already be familiar to those preparing Family Services.

The Welcome
The atmosphere for all-age worship is set before the actual service begins. Care needs to be taken that those responsible for welcome are not ignoring some of God's people; if the adults are greeted by name, the children should be too.

The opening of an act of corporate worship needs thoughtful preparation. It is likely to involve movement, as those leading come on the scene. This can be done in such a way as to signal the beginning of the service, without unnecessary pomp and ceremony. There may be a hubbub of conversation as people gather, which can be a positive sign of the fellowship that exists. However, it is worth giving some thought to means of quietening this in a way that does not deny the importance of fellowship but which raises a sense of anticipation and focuses attention on the presence of God. This is of particular importance in nurturing children in worship; even the very young will respond to the atmosphere around them. Music has a valuable part to play here, whether instrumental or sung. The first words spoken are important; they will either reinforce the sense of anticipation or kill it.

Music
Music plays a significant part in the corporate worship of a church. Whatever model of the church predominates, music approaches most closely to the principle of all-age worship. This needs to be acknowledged, and can be part of the process of helping others to catch the vision of all-age worship.

Singing in worship gives an opportunity for the active participation of all those present, whatever their age. The use of other instruments as well as the organ means that others can offer their musical gifts in worship. However, such music needs to be of a certain standard in order to enhance and encourage worship. Incompetent performance will not enable others to worship, whatever the age of the players. Sensitive musical direction and parts that are well within the scope of the player can ease this problem. It can be a valuable part of the mutual offering of all-age worship for a church to acknowledge the gifts of its younger members. Equally, everyone can join in parts formerly reserved for children. An invitation for everyone to join in the percussion should result in the rattling of car keys and the stamping of stilettos!

The choice of music for worship is an emotive issue and one that requires far more space than a booklet such as this allows. Music for all-age worship has to be chosen with particular care. Assumptions made about music suitable for children may not be valid. Children experience a range of emotions; they are not helped best by only hearing Christian songs that are bright and happy, in a major key. Nor should they patronized; there are better songs of praise for the whole community of faith to sing than 'Praise him, praise him, all you little children'. Care also needs to be taken over the selection of some of the worship songs of the renewal movement, which include a depth of emotional expression that is not yet part of children's experience.

There is sometimes an artificial division that assumes that modern music is for young people and traditional hymns for an older generation. This deprives the young of the resources of the best of hymnody, and fails to acknowledge the appeal that modern compositions can have for those of all ages. In choosing music for worship, it is better to set the goal of using good music and words, rather than concentrating too much on its age.

The approach that picks one childen's song, one for the youth group, and one for the old folk needs to be avoided. Care needs to be taken in the way in which hymns and songs are announced in all-age worship. To announce one item as 'the children's song' destroys the sense of being one community worshipping together; so does any suggestion that 'the children can join in the actions'. Resistance among older children to what it seen as babyish should be taken as a danger signal.

The Ministry of the Word
This phrase is used to cover the various methods by which the Word of God is proclaimed in worship. 'A Service of the Word' is deliberately vague about this, to allow for the flexibility of presentation that all-age worship will demand.

Part of the presentation of the Word will focus on the reading of Scripture. The passages to be read will be determined by the lectionary or the teaching syllabus. It is important from time to time to review the Scriptures read, to ensure that the congregation is receiving a balanced view. There is a tendency to limit the readings to one; there is then a likelihood of the Epistles and the Old Testament being neglected.

There is considerable scope for dramatised reading and for drama. The technique of response stories where those listening responding with key words and phrases[1] is particularly useful with a congregation of all ages.

There will be concern felt by some that the traditional presentation of a sermon is difficult to accommodate within all-age worship. Certainly the style of presentation needs adapting, but that does not mean that the gospel is watered down. Preachers need to cultivate a style that allows for plenty of illumination, in terms of illustrations both verbal and visual. This is not settling for second-best; Jesus himself taught in parables and pictures.

[1] For examples see Dave Hopwood, *Time and Again* and other publications, (5 White Rose Lane, Woking, Surrey).

Prayer

Consideration need to be given to how the community is enabled to pray together. So much of corporate worship is prayer, and that prayer takes different forms. The development of all-age worship will include a deepening understanding of the richness and variety of prayer. Here the structure of 'A Service of the Word', supplemented by the resources of *Patterns for Worship* will prove valuable.

Prayers that are said together have an important place in corporate prayer especially if they are used repeatedly, so that the words become so engrained that the depth of prayer goes beyond the words themselves. This applies not only to prayers such as the Prayers of Penitence and the Lord's Prayer, but also to responses, e.g.:

> The Lord is risen.
> **He is risen indeed!**

> Lord, in your mercy
> **Hear our prayer.**

Such memorization is an important part of spiritual formation in prayer, as is the experience of praying corporately.

For all-age worship, the material in *Patterns for Worship* is of value in directing the thoughts, particularly of those new to Christian worship. The responsive forms work well, provided that space is left between each paragraph to assimilate the material. If specific biddings are used, care needs to be taken to include all those present. This can be done by bracketing concerns, e.g. 'in our homes, our school, our work' so that the prayers have a validity for all those praying.

Shared leadership of corporate prayer can bring a sense of congregational participation. It has been common practice in Family Services to invite families in the congregation to lead the intercessions. This can be a positive step forward, in that the prayers reflect the concerns of those of different ages in that locality. Care needs to be taken that it is not exclusive, as can be the case if the invitation is offered only to nuclear families.

All the members of the congregation can be encouraged to express their contribution to the prayers. One method of doing this is by praying in small groups. Alternatively, subjects for prayer can be written down in groups, and brought to the prayer leader. A praise alphabet can be constructed by giving each group a letter of the alphabet to begin words that describe God. Once the concept of all the people being involved in prayer is grasped, the means of achieving this begin to follow.